THE PAINTERS WHO STUDIED CLOUDS

WILL KEMP

Cinnamon Press
INDEPENDENT INNOVATIVE INTERNATIONAL

Published by Cinnamon Press
Meirion House
Tanygrisiau
Blaenau Ffestiniog
Gwynedd, LL41 3SU
www.cinnamonpress.com

The right of Will Kemp to be identified as author of this work has been asserted by him in accordance with the Copyright, Designs and Patent Act, 1988. Copyright © 2016 Will Kemp
ISBN:978-1-910836-34-7
British Library Cataloguing in Publication Data. A CIP record for this book can be obtained from the British Library.

All rights reserved. No part of this publication may be reproduced, stored in a retrieval system, or transmitted in any form or by any means, electronic, mechanical, photocopying, recording or otherwise without the prior written permission of the publishers. This book may not be lent, hired out, resold or otherwise disposed of by way of trade in any form of binding or cover other than that in which it is published, without the prior consent of the publishers.

Designed and typeset in Palatino by Cinnamon Press. Printed in Poland.

Original cover design by Jan Fortune & Adam Craig from original artwork 'Sunrise over Gunnerside in Swaledale in Yorkshire Dales' by Matt Gibson © 'Honourableandbold' @ Dreamstime.com.

Cinnamon Press is represented in the UK by Inpress Ltd and in Wales by the Welsh Books Council.

Acknowledgements

Thanks to the editors of journals in which these and other poems have appeared: *Acumen, Aesthetica, Ambit, Angle, Cake, Dawntreader, Envoi, Equinox, Essence, Fourteen, The French Literary Review, The Guardian, Haiku Quarterly, The Interpreter's House, Iota, The Journal, Magma, The New Writer, The North, Obsessed with Pipework, Orbis, Other Poetry, Poetry Cornwall, Poetry News, Poetry Scotland, The Rialto, The SHOp, Smith's Knoll, The Times.*

Thanks too to Carole Bromley, Doreen Gurrey, Ann and Peter Sansom, Susan Richardson, John Glenday, John Billington, Tom Watson, Moniack Mhor, Ged, Jackie, Dave Nick, The Keats Shelley Memorial Association, Jan and everyone at Cinnamon.

The six lines quoted in 'Skies' are from 'The Trees', 'High Windows' and 'Cut Grass' by Philip Larkin in *The Complete Poems*, used with permission of Faber and Faber Ltd.

About the author

Will Kemp has won the Keats-Shelley Prize (2016), the Cinnamon Short Story Competition (2015), the Cinnamon Pamphlet Competition (2014), the Cinnamon Debut Collection Award (2010) and the Envoi International Poetry Prize (2010). Cinnamon Press published his collections *Nocturnes* (2011) and *Lowland* (2013), and his award-winning pamphlet, *The Missing Girl* (2015), and will publish his next, *In Another Life,* in 2019.

Notes

'The night I saw Vini Reilly': after *Requiem Again* by The Durutti Column, Factory Once, 1996.

'Gardening with John Clare': *wiz, crimpled* and *suthering* are East Anglian regionalisms Clare used for aspects of nature and weather.

Contents

I

Walking with Constable	11
Shopping with Elvis	12
Widor's Toccata	13
Driving to work at 5am while listening to Bach's Toccata and Fugue in D Minor	14
Air on the G String	15
View of Delft	16
Landscape with passing clouds	17
Returning song with song:	
i. The Flower Duet	18
ii. O Mio Babbino Caro	19
iii. Maple Leaf Rag	20
iv. Lark Ascending	21
v. Miserere	22
Night-shift	23
Night works:	
i. The Night Watch	24
ii. Starry Night	25
iii. Coalbrookedale at Night	26
The night I saw Vini Reilly	27
Tchaikovsky	28
Adagio for Strings	29
The Scarlet Sunset	30
Watercolour	31
The painters who studied clouds	32

II

The rowers	35
Fishing with Billy Collins	36
On England losing The Ashes	38
Moons and cricket balls	39
Just not cricket	40
Not just cricket:	
i. Rugby	41
ii. Swimming	42

iii. Golf	43
iv. Bowls	44
In praise of pipesmokers	46
Northern clouds	47
Trees	48
Taking down the beech	49
Listening to the wind	50
Lost on a moor	52
Kirk Gill Moor	53
November	54
Pheasant	55
The startled deer	56

III

In another life	59
Playing football with Keats	60
Gardening with John Clare	61
The first fairytale	62
Red Riding Hood	63
Persephone	64
Mrs Potifar	66
New	67
I want to be an extra in a film by Truffaut in which nothing much happens	68
Desert Island Discs	69
Reel to real:	
i. Toad	70
ii. Withnail	71
iii. Gatsby	72
The poets who watched the sky at night	73
Remembering Marie A	74
Bladerunner	75
Gloomy Sundays	76
Skies	77
The literary world:	
i. The Call of the Wild	78
ii. All Quiet on the Western Front	79
iii. As I Walked Out One Midsummer Morning	80

for Sibylle

The Painters Who Studied Clouds

I

Walking with Constable

I would have liked to accompany you to work, setting off
down a lane at that clang of the village school bell

to pass orchards and haycocks on our way towards
the untroubled skies of Suffolk, Essex and Cambridgeshire.

You would wear a high-collared coat, smile at my offer
to carry your easel and satchel, its pouches crammed with

notebooks, brushes, bottles, pens—maybe some apples
and cheese, a cob of bread for rough sandwiches.

Crossing a stile near East Bergholt, we would join
the towpath by the meandering Stour—you pointing out

those limestone clouds beyond the church-tower
at Stratford St Mary, likening them to some seen as a boy

from a tree on your uncle's farm, their bulk coasting over
the Fens to peel in two like a shoreline forming an inlet.

With a puzzled look I would try to picture them too—
wondering how often you must have looked up

at some flotilla churning and crumbling over the vale—
then watch you behold that gilded opening above:

the distant shafts of light spread down in a fan,
your face lifted towards the sky with all its possibilities.

Shopping with Elvis

I do the choosing, he pushes the trolley. Found it
embarassing at first—white glitter catsuit,
lapels bigger than the flaps on a cardboard box.
No dress sense at all. And that dancing in the aisle,
expecting everyone to do the Jailhouse Rock.
It's the way he is. Thank God people think
he's a tribute act. But last week one old lady knew.
Spotted him noting a special on some slippers.
Ya can do any thin bu lay offa ma blue suede shoes,
he started, off again. *That were Elvis,* I heard,
whisking him away, as her friend gasped: *Ye never!*
Wish he wouldn't do that. Though I quite like it
when he leans over to the check-out girl,
lowers his shades and says, *Thanyaverymuch.*

Widor's Toccata

Such is the profusion of intricate notes
in this wedding march for the organ
that only an octopus could be expected
to touch all the keys and pedals at once—

tentacle crossing over tentacle, tips looping
this way and that to pull out the stops—
though the octopus concerned would be
no ordinary mollusc from the sea-bed,

but one trained at the Royal Academy
in London or Stockholm
before joining a distinguished orchestra
such as the Berlin Stadtskapelle,

always looking so refined in those tails
and that white crepe bow-tie,
his head a grey balloon
nodding pensively in time with the tune

then acknowledging the applause
and calls of *encore* without a sound—
for this octopus would be nothing
if not an octopus of few words –

finally sliding off sideways
during the standing ovation,
with only a trail of brine across the boards
to show he'd been there at all.

Driving to work at 5am while listening to Bach's Toccata and Fugue in D Minor

I peer outside then flinch from the headlights' glare,
a movement not dissimilar to the quirks and winces
of Klaus Kinski in *Nosferatu the Vampyre*,

a role he must have relished with his long skull face,
talon hands, that silent movie leer—which makes
me think how I have missed my true vocation:

that, far from another day of filing and taking
an interest in the colleagues' children, I could be
waking in a crypt or creeping up some stairs

for audiences to marvel at my hunched shadow,
the believable way I shunned the dawn—
not once overdoing the recoil with a cat-like hiss,

but always maintaining the realism
of a much maligned and misunderstood bat
resigned to the eternity of that hollow, frozen stare.

Air on the G String

Just for the record I might as well say now
that I've always found it hard to resist

the image of Bach putting down his quill
after completing this famous score,

first taking off his dusty coat then
those breeches, tights and buckled shoes

to celebrate the glory of its creation
by strolling from the Liepzig Kaffeehaus

to the rococo Church of St Thomas
in only a G-string and that lofty grey wig.

View of Delft

after Vermeer

So realistic is this painting of the brick houses
and gabled Oostpoort reflected in the canal
that you can hear those two women talking

in the foreground—one recalling points
of note from the pastor's sermon on Sunday,
the other observing that the breeze brushing

her black dress and white bonnet would
not be unwelcome when drying linen sheets
or beating the mistress's carpet—

both pausing to agree that even the master
drawing the scene would struggle to depict
the fullness of this fast-flowing sky:

that pewter cloud darkening the Zuidwal,
its roof-tiles glinting from a recent shower,
and those lighter clouds clearing toward

the blue beyond to let the sun infuse
the distant tower of the Nieuwe Kerk
with the infinite power and majesty of God.

Landscape with passing clouds

If I could be anyone on this late afternoon
in autumn, it would be a landscape painter
from the early nineteenth century drawing
this view of the Wharfedale valley —

Turner perhaps on his first tour of the north,
looking more like a conductor than an artist
in his black waistcoat and white shirt
with that rough Eton collar.

I would begin by scaling off the distance
between those limestone fists on the ridge,
working down past the scree and woods
to the green velvet fields and dry stone walls,

plotting each landmark in a series of dots
before attending to those cows standing
in the river, that single pine above
the russet tree-line like a statistical outlier.

Only then would I add in the tones,
cross-hatching the shadows and hollows,
highlighting surfaces with Titanium White
to give the features form and light,

all the time asking whether the final work
should show that floral pattern of clouds
at dawn or in the softness of dusk —
just as, in fact, they are right now.

Returning song with song

i. The Flower Duet

If ever there were a piece of music
that lived up to its title—

the female voices intertwining
like sweet pea around a trellis

in summer—then this kaleidoscope
of notes must surely be it,

though the same harmony is
hardly true of my garden—

weeds thrust up, bushes shorn
on an industrial scale,

the lawn desecrated by the dog
digging holes and cocking his leg—

every plant seeming to wail:
Why is it you hate us so much?

ii. O Mio Babbino Caro

Even though I can't speak a word of Italian,
I can tell by the desperate soprano
that life isn't exactly on cloud nine right now,

so it comes as no surprise to learn
from a translation of Puccini's libretto
that she will throw herself into the Arno

unless her father lets her marry
the man she loves—which makes me realise
how lightly I got away with that question

to my wife's dad standing on the landing
in just his shorts and vest,
more interested, it seemed, in talking about

his defunct computer and the outcomes
of English battles, addressing me throughout
by the name of her ex.

iii. Maple Leaf Rag

If I could play piano, this piece would be
the tune, just as it was my mother's, sitting
at the harp-case of her Steinway Grand
on sunlit mornings, fingers tap-dancing over
the keys, head nodding like a metronome
while she sang *Da-da-da-dada-dadadadada*
under her breath, as if trying to perk up
the house or stop the gloom spreading from
my father's room as he pored over a lease
or contract, blocking out the brisk notes
being handed out across the hall;
her playing so natural, up-beat, defiant.

iv. The Lark Ascending

after Vaughan Williams

How well the violin
spirals up and quivers

like a lark struggling
to sing in the wind—

constantly faltering,
buffeted back,

yet always regaining
its speck of sky

to continue that call—
the rising orchestra

following the sound,
as if responding

like a mate returning
song with song.

v. Miserere

To listen to it now, four hundred years on
from the first hushed note Allegri penned
rising to that last grief-wrenched wail, is to see

the choirboy faces in the Sistine Chapel
as their voices weave towards the heaven
of Michelangelo's monumental ceiling,

and understand why pope after pope had it
banned from the ears of the world,

since God would be sure to hear, angels moved
to handle the passage of unworthy souls,

so that even I might ascend that same space,
passing Adam's crooked finger pointing
the way to the daylight of St Peter's Square,

then further still, clearing the doves circling
the dome, drifting upwards and far above,

turning slowly in a spiral of unfiltered light
like a diver coming up for air,

to enter the thin blue of the upper world
and dissolve into that distant whey of clouds.

Night-shift

after Leonardo's drawings of a foetus

We do the job after dark, digging up
a few from the afternoon then carting
them back to Santa Maria delle Grazie.
God's work, he says, letting us in
at the side door. No questions asked,
except this girl here, sixteen at most,
with child: *She is from where?*
I shrug my shoulders, suppress
those flailing hands at the fountain
by the Ospedale degli Innocenti.
Then look him dead in the eye:
Is she not exactly what you asked for?
He nods then pays. But I want more:
the drowned ones are heavier to carry.

Night works

i. The Night Watch

after Rembrandt

Even though my book on Holland tells me
this work marks a turning point in western art,
I can never look at its cluttered call to arms—
the dog barking at a drum, the cavalier waving
a guild's silk flag for no reason—without noting
that boy's distracted look as his pike clatters
into those leaning against the darkened hall,
an old-timer fumbling with his father's flintlock,
not quite ready yet. And somewhere there,
the voice of the portly captain, growing hot:
I cannot run a troop of men on ancient helmets, guns.
There's only one thing for it—to go to City Hall
and demand proper muskets, breast plates, swords—
for his lieutenant in the dandy hat to drawl:
Yes, I see sir. But do you really think that's wise?

ii. Starry Night

after van Gogh

the village sleeps
beneath hills drowned
by waves of blue

its spire a thorn
like the cypress trees
twisting up to

the rolling fireballs
of stars and clouds
only he could see

iii. Coalbrookedale At Night

after de Loutherbourg

Orange clouds froth up
by a soot-black silhouette of chimney stacks
in a surge of hell-born fire—
bellowed flames spitting yellow cinders,
as if a sorcerer had cast
saltpetre into that caldera
beyond the scarlet heaps of ash and clinker.

No stars or moon; no rustic swain calling
to his love below her bower.
Just the roar of an open forge—so hot
that men on the scorched red earth
can only stand back and watch
as rolling smoke engulfs
the tree-stripped slopes in a haze of sulphur.

And everywhere that blood-red glimmer
of reflected light basting
even the foreground figures—
the skulking dog,
that harnessed team heading out the scene—
night turned day, the world ablaze,
everything so terribly and utterly changed.

The night I saw Vini Reilly

he was playing alone in a pool of light—
fragile, blessed, *diminuendo*—
acoustic notes flowering into the air.

Just him and me, it seemed,
the chords twisting up into other worlds:

running through the garden as a boy
to escape a tickling by my mother,

going to sleep in winter
with my first proper girlfriend Boo,

and the day I heard *Requiem Again,*
at once seeing a full moon,
some oyster-shell clouds streaming on below.

Tchaikovsky

I can never listen to his Fourth without seeing
scores of Cossacks and hussars hurled into
the Battle of Smolensk or Poltava—

that trumpet calling men to make a stand,
take the fight back to the enemy,
bursts of drum-fire beating them down—

a scene he must have pictured too
banging the notes out on an upright piano
in a bare room at the Conservatoire,

wire glasses reflecting the frenzied score,
certain this piece would cruise through
the Winter Palace, find favour with the Tsar,

a future wave of violins crowding out
the threats from his estranged wife,
those thoughts about the First Cello—

that spark of a smile, the way he worked
the neck, how he might receive touches,
overtures—all swiftly countered by the risk

of rebuff and ruin, the rest of the orchestra
coming in now with that raging finale
in the only world he could control.

Adagio for Strings

Whatever sadness is not here is too sad to speak of,
as if every death or break-up was followed by
this slow flow of violin and cello,
and whatever restraint you showed gave way
to that silent howl of despair, the bitterest of tears.
You remember the one you loved from walks
through fresh fields, afternoons in sunlit rooms,
and the darkness that came after—so much unsaid,
unfulfilled, that will never now be resolved—
and think how Barber must have been there too,
knowing that in life there must always be
light and dark, though rarely in equal measure.

The Scarlet Sunset

after Turner's watercolour of Rouen

In the half-light,
a river is winding
towards a bridge
in the distance,
a thick blue mist
above and below
the sycamore red
of the evening sky.
Traces of towers
ghost into the dusk
of a faint wash
over gouache—
a pumpkin sun
already sunk into
the autumn haze.
Its reflection snakes
through the water
like the squiggle
of a signature,
the first sketch
having become
the work itself.

Watercolour

after Turner's sketches of Venice, 1819

Beyond the lagoon,
a low band of blue—

oblique, *sfumato* –
the city a mumble of towers, roofs—

the Campanile, that *duomo*
surely Santa Maria della Salute.

No silverpoint or ink,
just clouds flecked red

in an echo of those browns
along the foreshore.

And everywhere
the sky rinsed outwards

with that pale wash
of morning light.

The painters who studied clouds

From my window I am watching the sky drift by
in white and grey across the blue,
with dabs of lemon-yellow here and there,
where the sun glows a while
but never quite comes into view.

It reminds me of the painters who studied clouds,
no camera to catch the changing scene,
sitting alone in a field or tied
to a mast in some howling storm,
rolling sea and sky into one great swirl.

How quickly they must have worked
in silverpoint or chalk,
sometimes snowblind from taking in the light,
hatching rounded shapes with shade
to give the sky its full-blown form and tone,

at others cursing it for cirrus clouds moving
slower than ocean whales,
to let a sweep of wash
beach on the wet paper or seep
into a distant summer haze.

I wonder then if they too wondered
at Constable's *Study of Clouds*,
with its bulk of greys and half-greys,
windswept with hurried brushes,
sailing across and out the frame,

seeing how he must have looked and looked,
until he understood
the light, tone and shapes as one —
then took them down at once,
knowing in a moment they'd be gone.

II

The rowers

They came through the lifting mist,

                eight blades skimming the water,

each man stretching forwards then

                heaving back on taking the catch,

the bow at once thrust on towards

                the hard yards of the Long Reach,

the crew pulling clear of that grey

                like a longship leaving the sound.

Fishing with Billy Collins

You warmed to the idea over a bottle of Merlot
sipped pensively in your study
with its angle-poise lamp, the ring-stained desk
more accustomed to coffee,

though it took a while longer to decide
where to go—you bidding for the absolute calm
of Lake Huron, me the white water
below Elk River Falls—

a matter settled in the end by the toss of a coin,
with you stating your preference for
this method of resolution
to the former practice of pistols at dawn.

It came as no surprise that hooks, floats, flies
had never been on your list of things to buy,

or for that matter, that neither of us had ever
gone fishing, though my father did try once
before I ran back to my mother.

No surprise either that you stopped
the camper van, then eased into a description
of the feather-soft yellows to be found
in this part of New England during the fall,

or that we arrived after dark, too late
to assemble the rods or man the canoe.

Too late in fact to do anything
but lay either side of a camp-fire
fizzing with books neither of us liked—

you hands behind head, feet up
on a log like the end of a sofa,
reassuring me that fishing was
rarely about fishing, and what the hell —

maybe it was as well to continue
with the day job and just look at the stars.

I was unsure if the sky was lilac-blue
or blue-lilac, though you figured
neither was a good call since it brought
to mind the coffee pots of ranchers in films.

Then quiet. The quiet that must accompany
deep-sea divers stepping onto the sea-bed
light as astronauts on the moon.

I wanted to ask how you'd like
to be remembered, if at all, thinking how
the Apache or Sioux might have named you
Heart of a Bear, Watcher of Clouds,

but by now I was drifting off,
falling into a dream that at first light
you slipped into the lake
as if it were the great pool of English itself

and had already swum a long way out,
your head a tiny speck spearheading
an enormous V of water
before finally disappearing out of sight.

On England losing The Ashes

I suppose it was too good to last,
but what sticks in my craw is knowing that
those successive successes only came

by way of that lucky position on the sofa
(arms folded, left leg crossed over right)
and eating a pear before every Test,

though clearly neither did the trick this time
down under—not shaving upwards either,
or doing the ironing on one leg.

So it is little use the critics blaming
the black hole of defeat on the players' form,
the lack of warm-up games,

or for me to feel some relief
that at least it's over and I do not have to
stand at a bar in Sydney enduring

the jeers of the cock-a-hoop locals
at my accent and paltry legs,
because I am now walking out the village

with the glum look of an old wet dog,
plodding through the driving sleet
like Captain Oates on the Ross Ice Shelf,

all too well aware that I failed to find
a winning ritual of any kind,
and that this latest drubbing is all my fault.

Moons and cricket balls

Moons look down on people up to no good
in bedrooms, pubs. Cricket balls can't wait
to be picked from bags of sweaters, gloves.

Moons think they're made from marble
and pearl. Cricket balls have no idea
where they're from, or why they get rubbed
with spit then smashed for six.

Moons do their own thing. They'd rather stay
far removed, frozen in monastic solitude.
Cricket balls want to get stuck in and hear
shouts for an LBW as clear as daylight.

Moons admire the glaze of empty streets.
Cricket balls love the rough and tumble
of matches—sliding stops, fumbled catches.

Moons are switched on. Know exactly
where they're going. Cricket balls end up
in hedges, ditches, apart at the seam—
remembering times they used to shine.

Just not cricket

I can't remember the state of the game
or who we were playing,
only that the sky had a slight haze
and I was standing at slip

when the small red biplane buzzed
out of the blue beyond the woods
like the crop-sprayer in *North-by-Northwest*,

then soared, looping the loop,
corkscrewing the air,
taking on the sun in a single climb
before cutting the engine to plummet back
like a steepling catch.

Open-mouthed, we watched.

Then at last, that buzz,
followed by more twizzles and swirls
before he vanished, non-plussed perhaps
with the lack of applause,

but serving a reminder nonetheless
that cricket is hardly ever just about cricket.

Not just cricket

i. Rugby

There are few things I look forward to more
in winter than pouring myself onto the sofa
to watch England play Scotland or France,

marvelling at the fly-half kicking from hand
to launch a siege-gun shell spiralling from
the field of combat, or standing firm

to catch another steepling garryowen
as a horde of quash-nosed warriors thunders
forward to belt him into the next life.

I like to think I understand the terms—
loose-head, blind-side, maul—and belong
to this tribe of strong and beautiful men,

neatly overlooking those long walks from
massive defeats—a minstrel unaccustomed
to battle, a chieftain's disowned son—

whole afternoons trapped under some ruck,
gradually being flattened into
the ironing board cat in Tom and Jerry,

and most of all that same boy with stick legs
about to snap from the cold, whining
to Mr Barr: *Please sir, when can we go in?*

ii. Swimming

As a boy, I longed to dive into a pool.
I loved that blazing blue, like a tropical lagoon,
just asking to be smashed and divided
into lengths of butterfly and crawl;

lay awake at night holding my breath,
practising strokes on the bed —
my sister pointing out that if a life flashed past
I was probably drowning.

Neither of us could wait to watch
The Undersea World of Jacques Cousteau,
immersed in divers with spear-guns exploring
lost cities, reefs and barnacled wrecks;

I wanted to be one of those frogmen
shaking their wet hair then lounging around
like Knights of the Round Table
to discuss issues of pressure and depth.

I wouldn't be any trouble; I'd scrub the deck,
change my name to Philippe,
translate the clicks and creaks
of dolphin-talk into English and French —

at which point I'd be in, one of them,
falling backwards over the side
to glide to the sea-bed in a shoal of bubbles
wavering their way up to the light.

iii. Golf

I don't much care for golf,
in fact I only switched the TV on
to check the cricket, though soon
I was watching Tom Watson's round
as if the outcome depended on it—

not drawn by a love of sport
but the fairway smile of a boy
probably bullied for his freckles
and copper hair, that silent *thank you*
to hill after hill of standing applause.

A wish perhaps to see history made
without histrionics, or victory pass
for once to the most deserving,
as if a win here could somehow
right the wrongs of the world.

In the end, the putt faded wide.
He gave a rueful nod, as if it had
been a tough day at the office,
then half-raised a palm to handle
the collective grief of the crowd.

And at once came the drive to put
the record straight: Watson didn't
lose, he almost won, at fifty-nine—
though looking at that smile,
you might have thought he'd done it.

iv. Bowls

The sun is about to slip over the hill
as the game is drawing to a close,
with only a four left standing,
their shadows felled across the green.

How unhurried, how unconcerned
with fads and fashions they are
in their flat caps and sensible shoes;

how uncombative too
with those occasional winks and nods
to members of the opposing pair.

Indeed there are no hi-fives here,
no wild celebrations with players
hollering and leaping into the air;

no need for any slo-mo either,
or ra-ra girls in pink skirts
and white boots shaking pom-poms
while chanting *Let's Give 'Em Hell*.

As it is, one of them gives
a thumbs-up by the mat
before stooping to one knee
and bowling towards the jack,

the arm still outstretched long after
as if guiding the bowl along
the lifeline of some unseen path,

her spellbound pose like a movement
in Tai-Chi or a three day kunqu play
accompanied by the occasional *klonk*
of a two string lute.

From the deck chairs at the far end,
finished players look on
with a certain pride, less likely now
to scramble to the skies

than agree on the need to take
the weight off their feet
and that *you can't beat a good cup of tea,*

though now and then someone throws
a curveball into the conversation
by asking where to buy a walking stick
or a high-backed chair.

Doubtless none of them would have been
seen dead doing this fifty years ago,
yet nobody seems to mind

that in the time it takes to bowl
you could count the leaves
of an ancient oak or write a thesis on
pastimes in the sixteenth century.

And, as a motorbike hares off
past the hedge on the other side,
the opponents continue to take their time

like Sir Francis Drake before sailing
from Plymouth harbour to defeat
the Spanish Armada, knowing
that life is a marathon and not a sprint.

In praise of pipe-smokers

You hardly come across them nowadays,
sweetening the air with wafts of Cherry Rub
whilst strolling back to work from lunch
or reading The Times in the park.

Who would have guessed this forty years ago?
Back then, every man was a locomotive
breezing smoke: no conversation could be had
without him tapping a pipe on his shoe,

unclamping a tin to stuff some strands in
then lighting up in a series of puffs
as if keeping some sacred flame alive
(and all of this while still talking).

A pipe was the thing. You couldn't do
a crossword or mend a bike without one,
let alone solve a murder or have worked for
the Intelligence Service at Bletchley.

You didn't need to wear glasses and ask
smart questions in the pub; it was enough
to know your name was Reg or Bob
as you pondered the Bodyline Series

then made a point jabbing the air
with your pipe, its trail of smoke oozing out
like a genie from a lamp as you exuded
an assurance that all was right with the world.

Northern clouds

I like to watch them in the Dales—
blooming white and scudding grey,
swirling by or smoking off into the blue.

Take these, for instance, sliding past
the sun to make a forest of shadow
on that hill before revealing
the clear-fell of the morning sky,

or those yesterday—a row of puffs
above some invisible train,
each one moving slow as cows

before turning into the former shapes
of France and Germany as if mapping
the sky with the power shifts
of the late nineteenth century,

then sailing towards that haze
of light and twinkling rain,
their gradual drift a kind of letting go.

Trees

I can never decide when I like them best:
summer perhaps, green and full-blown,
prompting that wonder as to how
an artist could depict so many leaves,

or autumn, with memories of my mother,
who loved to watch the pale browns
of the distant Dales flame up
in the ripened light of the dying sun,

though walking today by frozen fields
in a gale, I know it has to be winter—
not for those pen and ink drawings
of bare branches in the woods,

but the tree-tops jostling the hurried sky
like the raised pitchforks
of a peasants' army about to throw off
the yoke of some vast, imperial power.

Taking down the beech

He stood on the lawn in a harness, reading
the stages between its splices and branches,

then hoisted himself up, chainsaw grumbling
while dangling from the tail of a rope below

before zipping into the bark, spraying sawdust
like sparks from a lathe, a creak leading to

a fan of leaves sweeping down to earth,
followed swiftly by another, and another,

until only he remained attached to the trunk,
taking in that new view of the whole valley.

Listening to the wind

I hardly ever get up late, but this morning
in October I am languishing in bed
with the window open, drifting in and out of sleep,
listening to the wind rise and fall--

one minute whorling its way through
the sail-tops of trees, the next hushing the street
like a tide dissipating across a shingle beach.

I try to think when I last heard it gust,
buffeting the house before dropping to that moan
which skitters some dead leaves on the drive
then ghosts about the rattling door.

It must have picked up in Trinidad
or perhaps The Azores, streaming over
this speck of York en route to the Russian Steppes,

where the local dialect probably has
as many words for *wind* as the Inuits do for *snow*,
and in particular a name for that quiet roar
you find in a conch or blazing fire—

the same sound that artists once depicted
as a boy blowing his cheeks from the edge
of a map, and which must have attended
every shipwreck in the eighteenth century—

the brig foundering in rough seas,
long since blown off-course and taking on water
after the captain's decision to run with the storm,

his shouts now lost in the sweeping rain
as the stricken vessel lists to port
and the gale lashes spray off the towering waves
about to crash down on the gunwale, flinging

all hands overboard into the freezing swell
to clasp flotsam and mutter prayers,
with no hope of help, and miles away from sleep.

Lost on a moor

Cold. Mist. Mud. Rocks. Rain.

A path leads on, but back to

the same place again.

Kirk Gill Moor

It was a gift to be there that afternoon,
as the jeep rollocked into view
and the old man unbolted the boot—
four collies sprung from the back

then snaking through the bottom field
to his growls of *Rob, Jamie, come here!*
One slipped the pack to cover
the ground in a long sweep—

an anti-magnetic force pushing
that white mass uphill and out of sight—
the track lost in dust, the dogs
close behind, working the drive—

until the sheep stopped
by the open gate to demur,
unsure whether to enter the lower fell,
then tumbled in as one.

November

yellowing to yellow
a slow decay

leaves earthed in
olive-green
wet sand
clay

ash trees flayed

poplars
fishbones
against that sky

darkening
with those clouds

held back
from the farthest sea

Pheasant

I hear that hiccup-croak then spot
him darting across the lawn
like a squat pen-pot and quill

before clattering off
towards the Colonel's woods,
barely able to clear the wall

in his starched collar
and tweed jacket made from
all the colours of autumn,

cheeks red as a portly parson's
on hearing his wife say
the word *sex* during afternoon tea.

The startled deer

She bolted from the brake,
a rush of brown over the road
and into the winter sun.

I stopped in time
to see the velvet head,
black flecks on her back and stilted legs,
as she eased to a tip-toe trot,
then vaulted the ditch and hedge.

At once she was gone.

Though that outstretched leap
stayed suspended in mid-air.
The way she landed too,
light and soft, already moving off
towards the cover of the woods.

And now all around
that hush,
when men with spears, moving
through the light-streamed dark,
must have first paused
by some pale green dots of ash or elm

and felt the need to capture
those *n*-shaped leaps
on the limestone walls of caves.

III

In another life

I'd have been Hercule Poirot.
If you'd had a career in Planning, you'd understand why.
It's something about developers,
the excessively rich, spraying you in mud
on site visits as they drive past in their green Range Rovers.

And their houses. The landscaped grounds,
the scrunch of those gravel drives. I could get used to
invitations to the country—long breakfasts
of kidneys and kedgeree, whisky marmalade
on triangles of cold toast, a choice of Assam or Darjeerling.

I wouldn't mind finding the body of his lordship
pegged to the back of my door, blue tongue lolling out
like one of the foxhounds after a hunt,
or hearing that the unhappy heiress had been asked
by the butler to hold some dodgy wiring.

I would know that distant pop before the shoot
was one name less on the rich list, could even bear
the wayward son's views on the servants,
already suspecting that smidgen of cake would be his last
and was—how you say in English—a kind of *denouement*.

Playing football with Keats

He was better than the rest of us by far,
dinking inside or coasting down
the wing on one of those dreamy runs,

but easily distracted—always listening
to bird-calls, staring into space
with that Buster Keaton look.

On match-days he took no heed
of the touchline shouts to nobble
the opposition, cut a solitary figure

watching the sky instead of keeping
an eye out for some booming clearance,
the chance of a quick free-kick.

I last saw him standing by the stream
after a practice one October,
taking in the sage and mustard scene

of the orchard trees beyond the field,
gnats whirling in the dying light,
that low mist woven into the hedgerow.

Gardening with John Clare

He'd come round every other Tuesday, then walk
home through the fields at four. I loved to see
that look of wonder in the pale morning sun
as he tended some flowering beans or watched
thrushes flit and wiz down the chattering hedge.
The best times though were when we'd sweep up
the crimpled leaves then stand beside a slow fire
talking about a wren or robin he'd spotted nearby.
And just as he'd be saying if this was gardening
then nothing had ever suited him half as well,
with the clouds brightening and deepening above,
a suthering breeze would start up from behind
to scatter some fresh leaf-fall across the lawn,
making us saunter back and begin all over again.

The first fairytale

It is after dusk, and I am sitting outside
with the beer you told me not to open,

trying to make out the tree-top shapes
lining the hillside in various silhouettes—

a wolf's head, a scarecrow and arguably
two witches—now picturing too

some oaf trudging home from market,
the family cow sold but the inn's flat ale

having proved too good to resist,
and already hearing his wife call him

a good-for-nothing-with-straw-for-brains,
but not for once thinking his description

of that giant cloud might just give her
an idea on how to recover their money.

Red Riding Hood

Of all the woods in all the world
she had to walk into mine,
the one I'd marked and pruned,
made love in beneath the pines.

I should have known of course
that red meant danger,
how little girls don't talk to wolves
and never go with strangers.

As it was, I could already smell
that roast lamb, see the afternoon
slumped under a tree, picking
hair from between my teeth.

Just my luck, then, the woodman
brings the old dear's shopping—
and being a do-gooder, asks if
she needs any kindling chopping.

That's the way it was. I know
they'll have their version too.
All I ask is someone establishes
the facts; the rest I leave to you.

Persephone

There, by the river, a shawl with patterns of flowers—
Persephone's since she was a girl.

Demeter held it as if cradling a sleeping child—
hands closed like buds, mouth a little o—
at once breathed in hibiscus, jasmine, rose;
recalled those first steps in the lemon grove.

Fruit. Persephone always loved fruit.
Apple, melon, plum: names learnt by heart,
practised like a song. Bluebell, primrose too,
all those questions on how leaves and petals grow.

In no time she flourished: took cuttings from ash
and willow; could paint a green field yellow.

She was a natural, down-to-earth too—laughed
as she sprinkled seeds, helped ladybirds to leaves.

Just couldn't be kept in: would follow
the flight of swallows over hills, vales, fields,
forever finding new paths and streams.

But she'd return.

The one time she did go missing, Demeter found
her on ground lit blue by the moon—decided
then to make the shawl (even though
in truth the girl was always a little hot);

at once Persephone draped it round and hugged
her mother—then promptly asked
if she could now stay out till dawn.

If she would only answer her name,
Demeter could hold her again—touch that head
the way cows nudge their young to water.

Instead, she stared at the river, remembering
stories, dances, walks:
her smile, her songs, her warmth.

Mrs Potifar

It was the way he moved that caught my eye.
Strong arms, light feet, skimpy thong.
Smooth chocolate skin. And a slave.
Well, I ask you.

I'd watch him in Accounts, bent over
those figures. Good with money, you see.
So I began to count on him in chains
bending over me.

Had it planned—P away, the time of month—
and summoned him forth. *Undress*, I said.
He didn't, of course, so I undid my gown
and flung him on the bed.

Just then P came in. Thinking quick,
I burst into tears, quite sure
the doe-eyed act would do the trick.
A man's world indeed.

As for Joseph, he's back making bricks.
I've no regrets, in fact it made me stronger.
Life isn't a question of who has power,
but simply how you use it.

New

I'm sitting at a desk on my first day with the firm
in a classic position of work—hands on knees,
face staring ahead out the window—

a cosmonaut waiting for take-off,
a pharaoh posing for his monumental statue
to be carved from the rock-face at Abu Simbel—

when a shout of *Oliver!* outside reminds me
of the 'sixties musical and how popular
that name is nowadays, unlike the genre.

Yet how sumptuous those films were—
Half a Sixpence, Chitty Chitty Bang Bang—
up-beat extravaganzas of sound and colour,

with nobody minding Kipps or Fagin slipping
into a song and dance routine, as if an orchestra
were always playing around the corner—

so that even now the Chief Exec might begin
his induction talk at ten by singing
Consider Yourself One of Us while waltzing me

onto the street followed by Accounts and IT—
men lifting girls in the air then twirling round
lamp-posts and mildly surprised passers-by—

the mind's camera rising in one tracking shot
to reveal a kaleidoscope of swirls
like roses blooming on speeded up film,

with everyone joining in the final chorus
before raising their outstretched arms
and shining faces towards the brilliant blue sky.

I want to be an extra in a film by Truffaut in which nothing much happens

not the young scruff at the *Café de Floré*
brooding over Sartre's *Nausea*
in a blur of Gauloises smoke

as his pretty girlfriend snaps
the passers-by reflected in the window
and asks why he looks so sad,

but the nondescript man behind
reading the early edition of *Le Parisien*
in those Yves St Laurent glasses

before ordering another café noir
then throwing his hands up
at the gastronomic size of the bill.

It goes without saying my hair would
be grey, clothes black and white,
all doubts and fears forgotten,

having long since mastered French
and swapped a career in Planning for
the stage-name *Jean-Luc Dubois*,

and that after lunch I'd take a stroll
under the rustling plane trees
lining the Boulevard Saint-Germain,

musing how this existence seemed
so fantastic, so insouciant,
that I must be living in a *belle époque*.

Desert Island Discs

Sir Bradley Wiggins is on the car radio selecting
the eight tracks he'd play if washed up
before those coconut trees and elegant palms —

a choice that includes *Rock N Roll Star* by Oasis,
the riff of which must be to rock music
what Long John Silver is to pirates —

when it occurs to me that I've never taken
a CD on a plane, and can think of
few things less likely than surviving
the obliteration of the crash only to come round

in the inter-tidal zone and behold
a complete music system half way up the beach —
black speakers encrusted with sand,
amp controls being twiddled by inquisitive crabs.

And if the improbability of these factors were
not enough to send the actuary in me
into a state of apoplexy, how had it got there
in the first place, in perfect working order,

and just what power supply would be used
in a place where the height of technology is
sending a message in a bottle out to sea?

How much better then to take those books
stowed away for the bliss of retirement
or even that great death-bed read —
The Great Gatsby, Hamlet, Asterix in Britain —

a mini library to dip into while waiting for
the drone of the search-plane, each paperback
buckled a little from drying too quickly in the sun.

Reel to real

i. Toad

If I were Toad in his cravat and summer tweeds,
you would be Frog holding onto your hat
in the front of my new open-top Rolls
with a picnic hamper strapped to the back
as off we roared down the leafy by-lanes
of Surrey and Hampshire heedless of speed,
honking the horn at each of my crash-sites
and shouting, *Hurrah for British Racing Green!*

until we came to a charming spot by the river
heartily recommended by Moley and Rat
where I would crank up the gramophone player,
pop open the champagne then lie back
to blow smoke-rings for you with my cigar
and say, *What a lovely Froggie you are.*

ii. Withnail

He thinks of the afternoon he called for
the finest wines available to humanity
in a tea-shop in The Lakes,
the time they legged it from the boozer
after declaring, *What FUCKER said that?*
on being called a ponce—
only to turn round to face
that twenty-three stone Irish builder.

But today there is just a wire-mesh fence
between him and the staring wolves
at London Zoo, his friend gone
in the hopeless rain, leaving
him with the sobering thought
of how he will never now play The Dane.

iii. Gatsby

Sometimes on summer evenings like this
when the light is rich and musky, I catch
a glimpse of him on his lawn by the pool,
laughing with Daisy. Only a week before,
this had been his dream; a week later he'd
be dead and she gone, off to another party
and all that jazz. I lived the high life once,
but deep-down knew it couldn't last.
This is his time then, the evening belongs
to him; not those beautiful girls with their
dazzling smiles, their flimsy words of love.

The poets who watched the sky at night

What were they like—Lu-Yu, Yang-Ti, Kojiju—
sitting by their bamboo house under the moon,

unable to sleep, reflecting on that pale flower
in the stream which cannot be caught in a jar?

Did they use lanterns or the brightess of the dark
to stir those brushes as pine cones dropped

in the jade woods by Yen Chao, then sleep by day
dreaming of the flight of moths in silk light?

And in those small hours, did they draw water
from the well with two faces, thinking how

the stars flicker like camp-fires across a plain
or blossom borne away on the Spring River?

Remembering Marie A

translated from Brecht

One clear blue day in September,
under a young plum tree,

I held my pale, silent love
like a precious dream.

And above us, in the summer sky,
a passing cloud I saw,

so white and high—
but even as I looked, it was there no more.

Bladerunner

I have...seen things you people wouldn't believe...
       —Rutger Hauer

Open-mouthed I've watched it a dozen times,
not once tiring of that dark atmosphere—
constant drizzle replacing the burnt-out sun,
Harrison Ford's down-beat drawl

and above all the human trait
of the replicants in seeking to prolong life—
a nuance that should make us all ponder
when we will go, and how:

during Sunday dinner perhaps or dozing
in a chair while the hand of Death points
a sleek finger-bone from the depth
of his black-hooded cloak,

yet surely not one of us will part
with half the magnificence
of Rutger Hauer himself as the fallen angel
with that neon riven hair—

bare to the waist, head bowed but pained
like *The Dying Gaul* as he fights
the unalterable fact his time has come—
though I wouldn't mind giving it a try.

Gloomy Sundays

Let us give thanks for those rainy afternoons
when there is nothing better to do
than bask on the sofa watching
The Belles of St Trinians or *Passport to Pimlico*;

for Stanley Holloway's bungling burglar
in *The Lavender Hill Mob*,
looking less like an arch-criminal
than an uncle stumbling back from the pub.

Let us not forget Hitchcock's bold move
to create some love interest in *The 39 Steps*
by handcuffing Madeleine Carroll
to Robert Donat in the face of certain death,

or the harpsicord jingle that accompanies
Margaret Rutherford's sorties for clues
in *Murder Most Foul* and made you wonder
if your gran could really be an amateur sleuth.

Let us overlook the plummy accents,
the stilted pauses, to imagine our parents'
dreamy gaze at the screen through
that cigarette haze at the pictures,

and rediscover a lost world
of simple plots and impeccable manners,
of slicked hair and double-breasted suits,
its black and white an endless source of colour.

Skies

I wish I could write like Philip Larkin
But have never come up with
An image anywhere near as good as
The trees are coming into leaf
Like something almost being said
Or been able to describe the sky
Without hearing his *deep blue air that shows*
Nothing, and is nowhere, and is endless.

I take the dog out across the fields
Hoping to nail the scene above,
Only to see *that high-builded cloud*
Moving at summer's pace,
Ending up at the pub with no better simile
Than feeling like an explorer
Reaching some far-flung corner
To discover someone else has got there first.

The literary world

i. The Call of the Wild

You can hear it now
                            long and low

alone
        as the moon clears

and the great unknown spreads out
        in silvered folds

the frozen lake a star-sprinkled glow

stalagmite trees pointing north
        like Inuit whalebone spears

where the shadows seem to move
        with something faint

but there

        through the powder snow

that percussion of panting

                  with padded feet

ii. All Quiet on the Western Front

It isn't so much our walk through the woods and vines
above the Rhine that brings the book to mind
as your remark that *Heimat* doesn't mean *homeland*

but rather *a place to which it is worth belonging* —
a notion those boys would have held true
moving up the line to Assmanshausen and beyond

before falling one by one in the dark of no man's land,
the mangled wire and broken trees lit up briefly
by distant flickers and spurts of fire.

Strange how I read it over thirty years ago
yet can still remember their names —
Kemmerich, Westhus, Meyer — those descriptions too:

gas snaking over the ground, sinking in the hollows;
Paul telling his mother the front was not so bad;
the screams of horses hit by the shelling.

No wonder he considered war such a hateful crime,
longed to hear flowing water, see sun-lit clouds
over orchards, meadows, fields;

and would have delighted in watching us pass
these beeches covering the slopes of the valley —
all the maps redrawn, the old order gone —

an Englishman and his German wife
counting the wayside plants from which to make jam:
bramble, rosehip, wild pear, sour cherry.

iii. As I Walked Out One Midsummer Morning

The cover alone made me
want to travel:

a barefoot boy with
blanket and fiddle

walking down a track
towards some hill-town

I imagined to be
Saragossa or Seville.

Not for me the family firm,
married by twenty,

but deserts, mountains,
jungles and towns—

finding Lake Titicaca,
Lhasa, Vilcabamba,

drinking from streams,
sleeping out in the open—

not once following
in anyone's footsteps.